Return Trip to Moses

By Atem

To Tristan

Copyright © 2023

The moral right to be identified as the creators of the work has been asserted by them in accordance with the Copyright, Designs and Patents Act 1988. All rights reserved.

No part of this book may be reproduced, stored in a retrieval system or transmitted in any form or by any means, electronic, mechanical, photocopying, recording or otherwise, without the prior permission of the authors.

Published by Red Feather Publishing

www.redfeather.com.au

Book Cover by Emma Powell

ISBN: Print 978-0-9942845-7-0

Infinite questions...

In the value of deeper Self

All answers slumber.

PART I

Introduction

Long, long ago there was a man called Moses, one of the Great Lord's most faithful servants. When Moses was already rather old, he was experiencing troublesome times with the folks he had brought out of Egypt on their way to the promised land.

So, one day, the Great Lord kindly asked him to pay him a visit on top of the mount where, at its foot, the people were just camping.

Moses, obedient as he was, prepared himself thoroughly, although we may assume that a silent sigh escaped his lips by the thought of undertaking such a giant climb.

Anyhow, he managed to reach the denoted place without any mishaps, which in itself was already a miracle, for there were a lot of loose stones on the mountain slope to be sure.

However, the Great Lord presented Moses with quite a forceful message for his people, which Moses—in case he should forget one or other detail—diligently engraved into a large flat piece of rock, for he hadn't thought it necessary to take with him some notepaper and a pencil.

The trip down was not easy either, especially with the extra load of his precious stone which Moses didn't want to lose, even if it would cost him his life.

It's sad to say, though, that the whole enterprise had taken much, much more time than had been anticipated, and when at last he had come down, people were not at all pleased to see him.

What had happened was that in the meantime, they had made a terrible mess of their lives, playing around with a silly calf made of gold, and moreover enjoying themselves immensely; can you believe it?

Seeing all this, Moses grew very angry indeed, and he had great difficulty in restraining himself as, before anything else, he had to inform his people of the ten not-to-be-mistaken orders the Great Lord had dictated to him.

So he pulled himself together, imposing silence in a stentorian voice upon the noisy gathering, and told them in no uncertain way about the given message.

This at least brought them a little back to their senses, for, after all, it came from a source they couldn't ignore.

But after some time, its powerful meaning started to wear off, and they began to remonstrate, arranging protest meetings, or whatever you might call it.

At that particular time, long, long ago, people didn't completely realise what they were doing, but we, more enlightened people entering into a new age, understand the situation jolly well.

More's the pity, but by giving someone an order, and expecting it to be obeyed, the absolute opposite always seems to take place; see for instance, Adam and Eve.

And after thousands of years, the Great Lord, having reached the outside of enough, made another call on Moses who, by now, although liberated from his commitments, was all the more pleased to render his services.

"This time," the Great Lord said to Moses, "this time I would strongly advise you not to descend from the mountain to their level, not under any conditions. For this time, after they've been able to correctly answer the questions I'd like you to present to all the people of the earth, they must climb the mountain themselves and hand them over to you personally."

"Sort of a quiz you mean?" asked Moses.

"Call it what you want, I don't mind," said the Great Lord, "as long as the result is satisfactory."

"I'll do my best," said Moses, "it's quite a job, but I'll do my best."

Then, as an after-thought, he said: "Would it be an idea to make up the questions in Haiku verse form*, for that's short and to the point, you see."

"Fine, fine," said the Great Lord, "but hurry, for the time is growing rather short."

* Haiku, an ancient Japanese verse-form, consisting of seventeen syllables: 5 – 7 – 5.

And so it happened.

And all the people of the earth one day found their questionnaire in their letterbox.

They no longer remonstrated, for they were no longer forced into obedience.

And answering the questions out of their own free will was actually great fun. All the more so when they discovered that they knew all the answers, which made them feel rather good.

In their billions, they flocked to the mountain in order to hand over their completed forms to Moses.

And Moses stood waiting for them on the highest peak of the mountain, surrounded by a large group of children who, with beaming faces, took delivery of all the forms, and fed them into a giant computer.

Mind you, the greatest wonder of it all was that in actual fact, every single participant won first prize, consisting of being allowed to live in a new world where peace and happiness reigned.

Where there were no more wars.

Where everybody cared for everybody because they no longer thought first of themselves.

What they did not yet fully realize was that they themselves, each one of them, had brought this new world into existence, simply by answering truthfully and living up to the questions Moses had posed to them.

Yes, so simple it was.

And Moses smiled happily, knowing that the Great Lord at last was able to have a smile on his face as well.

PART II

The Questions

1

What greater challenge

Than trying to overcome

The problems of life?

2

If mankind wants peace

Shouldn't we begin with ourselves?

The one solution.

3

To make all wars end

We must concentrate on peace.

Shall we all take part?

4

Can't we try bringing

A new world into being?

It just takes effort!

5

We can't enjoy life

Because of our commitments.

Why not live simply?

6

Between the nations,

Can't we try to find a point

Of conformity?

7

Isn't life worthwhile

When we feel responsible

For every moment?

8

Is it not high time

For facing reality?

Do we close our eyes?

9

Are we not aware

Of the enormous impact

Music has on man?

10

Are we not aware

Of the powerful impact

Movies have on man?

11

Are we not aware

Of the tremendous impact

The press has on man?

12

May we expect then

A sane world for our children

When we fail to choose?

13

Hasn't time arrived

For kindness in politics?

A relief for all.

14

One thing we forget

Which should be our main aim:

Where is our humour?

15

Without intention

We hurt each other so much.

Hi, how about it?

16

Politicians thrive

On ego satisfaction.

Are we so docile?

17

Isn't time ripe for

A wise man—like Socrates—

To govern the world?

18

So often we hear:

'Oh, it doesn't affect me.'

Aren't we all in it?

19

Can't we see marvels

In every little detail

Of our given life?

20

Have we shown the world

That in the end we always

Chose light above dark?

21

To have or to be,

Is it hard to make the choice?

We can't avoid it.

22

All through the ages

We've never been without war,

Isn't that a challenge?

23

World population,

Grabbing of each other's land.

Is war the answer?

24

Have <u>all</u> parents tried,

Really tried to stop their child

From going to war?

25

Have <u>all</u> humans worked,

Really worked to stop their men

Being snared in war?

26

Will we continue

Teaching our children to kill?

Let's ponder on this.

27

Only very few

Can rightly stand on their own.

Are you one of them?

28

Our experience

Has taught us how to react.

Do we ignore it?

29

Who made the sky blue,

The flowers so beautiful?

What a fine question!

30

We say: 'We want peace,'

And leave it to the neighbour,

Oh, are you busy?

31

Is it right to be

Unfaithful to each other?

Root of destruction.

32

Hospitality,

Friendship, kindness and laughter.

Have we forgotten?

33

Sensuous people

Do not know what real love it.

How many lifetimes?

34

Our thoughts, here and now,

Determine the stage we've reached.

Are we satisfied?

35

It was meant so well

To create Adam and Eve,

Did we destroy it?

36

On remembrance day,

Re-enacting past events.

What about today?

37

In the coming age

The world needs new-age people.

Are we strong enough?

38

Strong is not enough.

Why not work to reach the goal:

Peace and happiness?

39

If not you and I

Dare to take the first great step,

What chance does man have?

40

Yahweh just wanted

To protect us from ourselves.

Did we ever learn?

41

Moses just wanted

— — — — — — —

— — — — — ?

42

Buddha just wan —

— — — — — — —

— — — — —?

43

Jesus just — —

— — — — — — —

— — — — —?

44

Mohammed — —

— — — — — —

— — — — —?

45

Many more wanted

To protect us from ourselves.

Do we need go on?

46

Don't you think, people,

We could have a better world,

We, all together?

47

Growing every day,

Growing closer to man's goal.

Do you feel it too?

48

Shall we sing a song

Full of joy and giving thanks?

This we won't regret.

49

Aren't we privileged,

Being part of a new world

We have helped create?

50

When the day arrives

For departure from this earth,

Can we say: 'I did'?

51

'Did I give it all?

All my strength, my heart, my love'?

Then our world is saved.

ALSO BY ATEM

The Book of Hatma

Dhawana

(Published by Red Feather Publishing)

The Book of Eron

The Book of Godfried. 1975, Uitgeverij de Fontein bv, De Bilt ISBN 90 261 3021 x (in Dutch)

Het boek van de Eeuwigheid. 1996, Uitgeverij Kairos, Soest, ISBN 90 70338 467/cip (in Dutch)

Mijn Hemel, wat nu? 1975, Uitgeverij de Fontein bv, De Bilt, ISBN 90 261 3017 1 (in Dutch)

www.ingramcontent.com/pod-product-compliance
Lightning Source LLC
Chambersburg PA
CBHW051553010526
44118CB00022B/2691